GUILT-FREE GIRL

DESSERTS

About Bonnie Marcus

Bonnie Marcus launched her stylish stationery company, the Bonnie Marcus Collection "where fashion meets paper®," in 2002 from her dining room table, while expecting her first child. As a former wedding planner in New York City, Marcus was well-known for her event planning expertise and found there was a void in the stationery market in terms of fashion-forward stylish designs. She decided to combine her passion for fashion (having worked for designer Diane Von Furstenberg) with her love of event planning and her collection took the stationery industry by storm! Bonnie's stylish designs are now available in thousands of retail stores worldwide and celebrity fans include Cindy Crawford, Christina Aguilera, Britney Spears, Eva Longoria, Marcia Cross, and many others. Marcus has been recognized as a pioneer for women in business and is proud to be an established partner of the Breast Cancer Research Foundation® and Autism Speaks®. For further information about the company, please visit www.bonniemarcus.com.

Bonnie Marcus Collection

GUILT-FREE GIRL

DESSERTS

DELICIOUS FIGURE-FRIENDLY RECIPES FOR ANY OCCASION

Bath • New York • Singapore • Hong Kong • Cologne • Delhi
Melbourne • Amsterdam • Johannesburg • Shenzhen

This edition published by Parragon Books Ltd in 2013 and distributed by

Parragon Inc.
440 Park Avenue South, 13th Floor
New York, NY 10016
www.parragon.com

Project managed by Cheryl Warner
New recipes and additional text by Robin Donovan
Photography by Ian Garlick
Internal design by Lisa McCormick

ISBN 978-1-4723-2979-0

Printed in China

Notes for the Reader

This book uses standard kitchen measuring spoons and cups. All spoon and cup measurements are level unless otherwise indicated. Unless otherwise stated, milk is assumed to be whole, eggs are large, individual vegetables are medium, and pepper is freshly ground black pepper. Unless otherwise stated, all root vegetables should be peeled prior to using.

Garnishes, decorations, and serving suggestions are all optional and not necessarily included in the recipe ingredients or method. Any optional ingredients and seasoning to taste are not included in the nutritional analysis. The times given are only an approximate guide. Preparation times differ according to the techniques used by different people and the cooking times may also vary from those given. Optional ingredients, variations, or serving suggestions have not been included in the time calculations.

Nutritional values are per serving or per item (for Makes…). Consult your physician before following any new diet or fitness plans.

Contents

The Guilt-Free Life

What girl doesn't want to eat her cake and look good doing it? Well, now you can with this guilt-free collection of recipes! The desserts in this book let you indulge in delicious sweet treats without any of the usual regrets as these recipes are all low in calories and low in fat. What could be more perfect?

If you thought you had to give up sinfully tasty desserts in order to look and feel healthy, think again. You can (and, as far as we're concerned, should!) enjoy delicious food—even amazing desserts—as part of a healthy lifestyle. The key isn't deprivation at all, but moderation. Pick your moments, watch your portion size, look for nutrient-dense ingredients, and choose desserts with the most intense flavors so that you get deep satisfaction from every bite.

From perfect little bites, such as our spicy Chai Tea Cookies made with whole-wheat flour, rich Fig & Hazelnut Biscotti, or superlight and tangy Lemon Meringue Cookies, to dinner party showstoppers, such as our oozy Mini Molten Chocolate Cakes and architecturally stunning Strawberry & White Chocolate Mousse Napoleons, the desserts you'll find here will satisfy your most intense cravings. Bursting with flavor, they'll never leave you feeling deprived. They are big on flavor, but each is surprisingly low in calories and fat.

We've got sweet treats for casual gatherings, quick snacks to satisfy a sweet tooth in a pinch, and elaborate desserts that are sure to be a highlight of any party. And the best thing is that with fewer than 250 calories per serving, each and every one will leave you feeling lithe and lovely and ready to take on the world. Come and join the guilt-free revolution!

The Perfect Little Bite

Chai Tea Cookies

INGREDIENTS
makes 30

½ cup firmly packed light
   brown sugar
2 tablespoons dry chai tea
   (about 4 tea bags)
¼ teaspoon salt
1 cup whole-wheat flour,
   plus extra for dusting
1 teaspoon vanilla extract
1 stick cold, unsalted butter

METHOD

1 Preheat the oven to 350°F and line a cookie sheet with parchment paper.

2 Put the brown sugar, tea, and salt into a food processor and process until the tea has been ground to a fine powder. Add the flour, vanilla extract, and butter and process until well combined and the mixture begins to hold together. If the mixture is too dry, add cold water, about ½ teaspoon at a time, and process until the dough just comes together. Turn out the dough onto a sheet of plastic wrap and shape into a log. Wrap tightly and refrigerate for 15 minutes.

3 On a lightly floured surface, roll out the dough to about ⅛-inch thick and cut into circles, using a round 2½-inch cookie cutter (or use the shape of your choice). Transfer the cookies to the prepared cookie sheet and bake in the preheated oven for 18–20 minutes, or until they begin to brown.

4 Remove from the oven and transfer the cookies to a wire rack to cool completely. Serve at room temperature.

Sesame, Marshmallow & Cranberry Squares

calories 124 | fat 5.3g | sat fat 0.6g | total sugars 12.3g | carbs 19g

INGREDIENTS
makes 20

1⅔ cups rolled oats
⅓ cup sesame seeds
3 tablespoons packed light
    brown sugar
⅔ cup miniature marshmallows
½ cup dried cranberries
½ cup honey
⅓ cup sunflower oil,
    plus extra for greasing
a few drops of vanilla extract

METHOD

1 Preheat the oven to 325°F. Lightly brush an 11 x 7-inch baking pan with oil. Line the bottom with nonstick parchment paper.

2 Put the oats, sesame seeds, sugar, marshmallows, and cranberries into a mixing bowl and stir. Make a well in the center, add the honey, oil, and vanilla extract, then stir again.

3 Press the dough into the prepared baking pan and level, using a metal spoon. Bake in the preheated oven for 20 minutes, or until golden brown and bubbling.

4 Let cool in the pan for 10 minutes, then cut into small squares. Let cool completely before turning out of the pan. Serve or store in an airtight container in a cool, dry place for up to two days.

Pecan-Butterscotch Bars

calories 224	fat 9.3g	sat fat 3g	total sugars 23.3g	carbs 32.6g

INGREDIENTS
makes 12
crust
cooking spray
½ cup firmly packed light
    brown sugar
4 tablespoons butter
½ cup whole-wheat flour
½ cup all-purpose flour
2 teaspoons water

filling
2 eggs
¾ cup firmly packed light
    brown sugar
1 tablespoon all-purpose flour
1 teaspoon vanilla extract
¼ teaspoon salt
¾ cup pecan pieces

METHOD

1 Preheat the oven to 375°F. Spray an 11 x 7 x 2-inch baking pan with cooking spray.

2 To make the crust, cream together the brown sugar and butter in a medium bowl, using an electric mixer. Add both flours and the water and mix until combined. Transfer the dough to the prepared baking pan and cover the bottom of the pan in an even layer. Bake in the preheated oven for about 12–15 minutes, until lightly browned. Remove from the oven, but leave the oven on.

3 While the crust is baking, make the filling. Beat the eggs, brown sugar, flour, vanilla extract, and salt in a large bowl with an electric mixer until well combined. Stir in the pecan pieces and pour the mixture over the warm crust in the baking pan. Bake in the preheated oven for 18–20 minutes, or until the filling begins to brown around the edges.

4 Remove from the oven and transfer to a wire rack to cool completely.

5 Cut into 12 squares and serve at room temperature.

White & Dark Chocolate-Dipped Strawberries

| calories 54 | fat 3g | sat fat 1.7g | total sugars 5g | carbs 6.3g |

INGREDIENTS
makes 24

4 ounces semisweet chocolate, coarsely chopped
4 ounces white chocolate, coarsely chopped
24 large strawberries

METHOD

1 Line a baking sheet with nonstick parchment paper. Put the semisweet chocolate and white chocolate into two separate double boilers or heatproof bowls, set the bowls over two saucepans of gently simmering water, and heat until melted.

2 Dip the pointed end of each strawberry into one of the melted chocolates and transfer it to the prepared baking sheet. Let cool for 1 hour, or until set.

3 Put each strawberry in a liqueur glass or on a plate and serve immediately.

Caramel Popcorn Bites

| calories 230 | fat 7.5g | sat fat 2.5g | total sugars 38g | carbs 44g |

INGREDIENTS
serves 8

½ cup granulated sugar
½ cup firmly packed light
   brown sugar
½ cup light corn syrup
2 tablespoons butter
1½ teaspoons baking soda
1 teaspoon salt
½ teaspoon vanilla extract
8 cups plain, air-popped
   popcorn

METHOD

1 Cover a large baking sheet with parchment paper or aluminum foil.

2 In a saucepan, combine the sugars, corn syrup, and butter and bring to a boil over medium–high heat. Reduce the heat to medium and boil, without stirring, for 4 minutes. Carefully stir in the baking soda, salt, and vanilla extract.

3 Put the popcorn in a large mixing bowl. Pour the caramel over the popcorn and stir to coat. Using two spoons, form the mixture into 24 balls, about 2 inches in diameter, and place them on the lined baking sheet. Let sit at room temperature for about 1 hour, or until firm. Serve at room temperature.

Crispy Chocolate, Fruit & Nut Bark

calories 153	fat 9.6g	sat fat 4.8g	total sugars 10.4g	carbs 15.5g

INGREDIENTS
makes 16

½ cup dried cherries
½ cup hazelnuts, chopped
12 ounces semisweet chocolate, chopped
⅔ cup crispy rice cereal

METHOD

1 Line a 9 x 11-inch baking pan with parchment paper.

2 In a small bowl, combine the cherries and hazelnuts and mix well.

3 Put the chocolate in the top of a double boiler set over simmering water, or use a heatproof bowl set over a saucepan of gently simmering water, and heat, stirring frequently, until the chocolate has melted. Remove from the heat and stir in the rice cereal.

4 Pour the chocolate mixture into the prepared pan and smooth it into a thin layer, using a rubber spatula. Immediately top with the cherries and nuts, sprinkling them evenly over the top. Press the cherries and nuts into the chocolate with the palm of your hand. Refrigerate for at least 1 hour, until completely set.

5 Break into pieces and serve at room temperature.

Lemon Meringue Cookies

| calories 73 | fat 0g | sat fat 0g | total sugars 17g | carbs 18g |

INGREDIENTS
serves 8

2 egg whites
⅛ teaspoon cream of tartar
pinch of salt
⅔ cup superfine sugar
finely grated zest of 1 lemon

METHOD

1 Preheat the oven to 200°F. Line a large baking sheet with aluminum foil or parchment paper.

2 In a medium bowl, beat the egg whites with an electric mixer on high speed until they are frothy. Add the cream of tartar and salt and continue to beat on high until soft peaks form. Gradually add the sugar and continue to beat on high for about 3–4 minutes, or until stiff peaks form. Fold in the lemon zest.

3 Drop the batter in rounded teaspoons onto the prepared baking sheet. Bake in the preheated oven for about 1½ hours, or until dry and crisp but not yet beginning to brown. Turn off the oven and let the cookies sit inside for another 30 minutes. Serve at room temperature.

Mocha-Filled Phyllo Cups

calories 183 | fat 6.5g | sat fat 3.5g | total sugars 19g | carbs 27g

INGREDIENTS
makes 8
phyllo cups
3 sheets frozen phyllo dough,
    thawed
cooking spray
1 teaspoon granulated sugar
halved strawberries, to serve
    (optional)

filling
4 ounces semisweet chocolate,
    chopped
3 tablespoons unsweetened
    cocoa powder
about 1 cup water
1 teaspoon vanilla extract
1 tablespoon instant
    espresso powder
½ cup granulated sugar
3 egg whites
¼ teaspoon cream of tartar

METHOD
1 Preheat the oven to 350°F.

2 To make the phyllo cups, carefully separate one phyllo sheet from the others, lay it on a work surface, and spritz it all over with the cooking spray. Sprinkle it with about one-third of the sugar. Lay another sheet of phyllo over the top of the first and repeat the steps until you have three layers, ending with a sprinkling of sugar. Cut the stack of phyllo sheets into eight rectangles, and place each rectangle into an ungreased muffin cup, pressing down to form a cup out of the phyllo. Bake the phyllo cups in the preheated oven for about 6–8 minutes, or until lightly browned. Remove from the oven and let cool in the pan for several minutes, then transfer to a wire rack to cool completely before removing from the pan.

3 To make the filling, put the chocolate, cocoa, and ⅓ cup water in the top of a double boiler set over simmering water, or use a heatproof bowl set over a saucepan of gently simmering water, and heat, stirring frequently, until the chocolate has completely melted and the mixture is smooth. Remove from the heat and stir in the vanilla extract and espresso powder. Remove the bowl from the saucepan and set aside.

4 In a small saucepan, combine the sugar with ½ cup water and bring to a boil. Cook, stirring, for about 5 minutes, or until the mixture begins to thicken.

5 Beat the egg whites in large bowl with an electric mixer until foamy. Add the cream of tartar and beat, gradually increasing the speed, until soft peaks form. With the mixer running, slowly add the warm sugar mixture. Increase the speed to high and beat until the mixture has cooled and stiff, glossy peaks form.

6 Whisk one-third of the egg white mixture into the chocolate mixture until it is well combined. Whisk in the remaining egg-white mixture. Transfer to a medium bowl and cover with plastic wrap, pressing the wrap directly onto the surface to prevent a skin from forming. Chill in the refrigerator for at least 1 hour.

7 Just before serving, scoop the filling into a pastry bag fitted with a large star tip. Pipe the filling into the phyllo cups, dividing it equally among them. Serve immediately, with halved strawberries if desired.

Live Life to the Fullest!

Live your life the guilt-free way! Eating should be enjoyable, so why cram yourself into a harsh dieting lifestyle that makes you miserable? You absolutely can enjoy an active lifestyle and be as healthy as you've always dreamed of being while eating delicious food—even deeply satisfying desserts such as the ones on these pages. These recipes are low in calories and fat, so there is no guilt!

The key to enjoying life to its fullest—including eating delicious, satisfying food—while staying healthy is moderation. If you swear off whole categories of foods, you run the risk of creating an obsession so intense that you'll spend your days thinking about nothing but buttercream frosting and chocolate cake. If, on the other hand, you call a truce with those "forbidden" foods and allow all things in moderation, you'll be able to satisfy those urges and move on, perhaps even have time and energy for a brisk walk or an invigorating workout at the gym. The guilt-free way is simple!

Make wise choices and you'll be on the right path. Our Maple-Nut Granola Bars make for a wonderful, protein- and fiber-packed treat. Eat just one and you get a ton of nutrition, not to mention enjoyment.

If a cheeseburger and fries is what you're craving, make it a turkey burger stuffed with spinach, herbs, and feta cheese. Switch the fries for baked sweet potato fries, which are full of vitamins. You'll end up feeling completely satisfied without wasting an entire day's worth of calories on one gut-busting meal.

If chocolate cake is the only thing that will do, try our Mini Molten Chocolate Cakes, which are flourless, relatively low in sugar, and full of rich, dark chocolate flavor. If it's cheesecake you want, try our Berry & Rhubarb Cheesecake Bars. They pack all the flavor and creamy, rich cheesecakiness you love in a lightened-up package.

And remember, being a guilt-free girl is all about having the food and flavors you love!

Maple-Nut Granola Bars

calories 200	fat 10g	sat fat 1.5g	total sugars 11g	carbs 22.8g

INGREDIENTS
makes 12

cooking spray
1½ cups rolled oats
½ cup chopped pecans
½ cup slivered almonds
½ cup maple syrup
¼ cup firmly packed light
    brown sugar
¼ cup creamy peanut butter
1 teaspoon vanilla extract
¼ teaspoon salt
2 cups puffed rice cereal
¼ cup ground flaxseed

METHOD

1 Preheat the oven to 350°F. Coat a 9 x 13-inch baking dish with cooking spray.

2 In a large baking pan, combine the oats, pecans, and almonds and toast in the preheated oven for 5–7 minutes, or until lightly browned.

3 While the oats and nuts are toasting, combine the maple syrup, brown sugar, and peanut butter in a small saucepan and bring to a boil over medium heat. Cook, stirring, for about 4–5 minutes, or until the mixture thickens slightly. Stir in the vanilla extract and salt.

4 When the oats and nuts are toasted, place them in a mixing bowl and add the rice cereal and flaxseed. Add the syrup mixture to the oat mixture and stir to combine. Spread the mixture into the prepared baking dish and chill for at least 1 hour before cutting into 12 bars. Serve at room temperature. Store in a tightly covered container.

Fig & Hazelnut Biscotti

| calories 182 | fat 7.3g | sat fat 2g | total sugars 14g | carbs 26g |

INGREDIENTS
makes 18

1 cup all-purpose flour
1 cup whole-wheat flour
½ teaspoon baking powder
½ teaspoon baking soda
¼ teaspoon salt
4 tablespoons unsalted butter, softened
½ cup sugar
¼ cup firmly packed brown sugar
1 tablespoon vanilla extract
1 tablespoon orange zest
2 eggs
¾ cup chopped, toasted hazelnuts
1 cup dried figs, chopped

METHOD

1 Preheat the oven to 350°F. Line a cookie sheet with parchment paper.

2 In a medium bowl, combine the flours, baking powder, baking soda, and salt.

3 In a large bowl, use an electric mixer to cream together the butter and sugars. Add the vanilla extract and orange zest, then the eggs, one at a time, beating after each addition. Add half of the flour mixture and mix until combined. Add the remaining flour mixture along with the nuts and figs. Mix until incorporated.

4 Turn out the dough onto the prepared cookie sheet and shape into two loaves, about 8 x 3 inches. Bake in the preheated oven for about 30–35 minutes, or until golden brown. Remove from the oven and let cool for 10–15 minutes. Reduce the oven heat to 325°F.

5 Slice the loaves on the diagonal into 1-inch-thick pieces and place them on end on the cookie sheet so that both cut sides are exposed. Bake for about 25 minutes, or until lightly browned.

6 Remove from the oven and transfer to a wire rack to cool completely before serving.

Superchilled!

Frozen Yogurt Cups

calories 26	fat 0.4g	sat fat 0.2g	total sugars 4g	carbs 4g

INGREDIENTS
makes 12

2 cups low-fat plain yogurt
1½ tablespoons finely grated
    orange rind
2 cups mixed berries, such
    as blueberries, raspberries,
    and strawberries, plus
    extra to decorate
fresh mint sprigs, to decorate
    (optional)

METHOD

1 Set the freezer to its coldest setting at least 2 hours before freezing this dish. Line a 12-cup muffin pan with 12 muffin cups or use small ramekin dishes placed on a baking sheet.

2 Mix together the yogurt and orange rind in a large bowl. Cut any large strawberries into pieces so that they are the same size as the blueberries and raspberries.

3 Add the fruit to the yogurt, then spoon into the cups or ramekins. Freeze for 2 hours, or until just frozen. Decorate with extra fruit and mint sprigs, if using, and serve. Remember to return the freezer to its original setting afterward.

Banana-Coconut Ice Cream Balls

calories 173	fat 10g	sat fat 5g	total sugars 12.3g	carbs 20g

INGREDIENTS
serves 6

3 ripe bananas
¼ cup evaporated milk
2¾ ounces semisweet chocolate, cut into small pieces
1 tablespoon canola oil
3 tablespoons shredded unsweetened dried coconut

METHOD

1 Peel and cut the bananas into small pieces. Put into a freezer-proof container and freeze for at least 2 hours. Transfer the frozen bananas to a food processor or blender and add the evaporated milk. Process until smooth and creamy. Scrape the mixture into a freezer-proof container, cover, and freeze for another hour or so, until the mixture is firm.

2 Put the chocolate and oil in the top of a double boiler set over simmering water, or use a heatproof bowl set over a saucepan of gently simmering water, and heat, stirring frequently, until melted. Place the coconut in a bowl.

3 Line a baking sheet with parchment paper. Use a small scoop (such as a melon baller) to create 2-inch balls of the banana mixture and set them on the prepared baking sheet. If the balls begin to soften, place them in the freezer for 15 minutes, or until they are firm again. Working quickly, spear an ice cream ball with a toothpick and dunk it into the melted chocolate, twirling to coat completely. Let the excess chocolate drip off, then transfer the ball to the bowl of shredded coconut and turn to coat lightly.

4 Place the balls on the parchment paper and continue until all of the ice cream balls are coated in chocolate. Place the baking sheet in the freezer for a few minutes, chill until firm, and serve immediately.

Eat the Guilt-Free Foods You Love!

A guilt-free girl wants the best of both worlds—delicious flavors and a healthy lifestyle! But eating healthy doesn't have to be an excruciating exercise in deprivation. It's really more about making good choices and smart substitutions. Think of it as a way to feel great, have more energy, and be happy, all while keeping your body as healthy as possible. Eating a healthy, guilt-free diet is just a matter of making everything you eat as good-for-you as possible without adding any empty calories.

Boosting the nutrition of your favorite recipes is really as easy as switching purses, or, more specifically, substituting whole grains—such as whole-wheat or brown rice flour, or even quinoa or amaranth flour—for processed white flour. Our Chai Tea Cookies and Pecan-Butterscotch Bars are perfect examples of how easy it is to boost nutrition without sacrificing flavor.

Substituting fruits and other natural sweeteners for refined sugar is another way to boost the nutritional content of foods, while also reducing their calories. Applesauce, pureed ripe pears or bananas, and agave syrup are great ways to sweeten food without a lot of empty calories (or scary chemicals). Our spicy and moist Lemon-Glazed Gingerbread Cake, for instance, is sweetened with applesauce.

Using healthy fats, such as those from avocadoes, olives, nuts, and seeds, also makes foods healthier without detracting from their appeal. Our Almond Cupcakes with Poached Pears, for example, get most of their richness from ground almonds (almond meal), which delivers a type of fat that may help to lower cholesterol and reduce the risk of certain illnesses.

By simply cutting down on saturated fats, such as butter and cream, you can give some of your favorite desserts a healthy makeover. Key Lime Pie made with fewer egg yolks (more egg whites), fat-free sweetened condensed milk, and nonfat yogurt is far lighter and healthier than the classic variety. Likewise, using egg whites in place of cream in chocolate mousse, as in our Mocha-Filled Phyllo Cups, is ingenious, even if we do say so ourselves.

If you want to be superextra clever, try adding a few "superfoods" ingredients that are densely packed with nutrients to your favorite recipes. For example, add a few tablespoons of ground flaxseeds to muffins or brownies, dried goji berries to a milk shake or smoothie, or chia seeds for a little extra crunch in your shortbread cookies.

Mochaccino Pops

(calories 69) (fat 0.5g) (sat fat 0.3g) (total sugars 12g) (carbs 13.5g)

INGREDIENTS
makes 6

1 cup cold 1% milk
1 teaspoon unflavored
    powdered gelatin
⅓ cup strong brewed coffee
    or espresso
¼ cup sugar
¼ cup unsweetened cocoa
    powder
½ teaspoon vanilla extract

METHOD

1 Pour the milk into a medium bowl and sprinkle the gelatin over the top. Let sit for about 5 minutes, or until the gelatin has softened.

2 In a small saucepan, heat the coffee over medium heat until hot but not boiling. Add the sugar and cocoa powder, remove from the heat, and whisk until the sugar and cocoa powder have dissolved. Add the vanilla extract.

3 Slowly whisk the milk mixture into the warm coffee mixture. Continue whisking for about 3 minutes, or until the gelatin has completely dissolved. Pour the mixture into six miniature ice pop molds, insert the sticks, and freeze for at least 4 hours or overnight. Serve frozen.

41

Red Wine Sorbet

| calories 166 | fat 0g | sat fat 0g | total sugars 22g | carbs 23g |

INGREDIENTS
serves 6

1 orange
1 lemon
2½ cups fruity red wine
⅔ cup firmly packed light
   brown sugar
1¼ cups water, chilled
2 egg whites, lightly beaten
fresh fruit, to serve

METHOD

1 Peel the zest from the orange and lemon in strips, using a vegetable peeler, being careful not to remove any of the bitter white pith underneath. Put in a saucepan with the red wine and sugar. Heat gently, stirring until the sugar dissolves, then bring to a boil and simmer for 5 minutes. Remove from the heat and stir in the water.

2 Squeeze the juice from the fruit. Stir into the wine mixture. Cover and let sit until completely cool, then strain into a freezer-proof container. Cover and freeze for 7–8 hours, or until firm.

3 Working quickly, break the sorbet into chunks and transfer to a food processor. Blend for a few seconds to break down the chunks, then, leaving the processor running, gradually pour the egg whites through the feed tube. The mixture will become paler. Continue blending until smooth.

4 Freeze for an additional 3–4 hours, or until firm. Scoop into six chilled glasses or dishes and serve immediately with the fresh fruit.

Lemon Buttermilk Sherbet

calories 176	fat 1.6g	sat fat 1g	total sugars 37.8g	carbs 38.6g

INGREDIENTS
serves 6

1 tablespoon finely grated lemon zest
¼ cup fresh lemon juice
1 tablespoon fresh lime juice
1 cup sugar
2 cups buttermilk

METHOD

1 If you are using an ice cream maker, freeze the insert of your ice cream maker for at least 24 hours.

2 In a medium bowl, combine the lemon zest, lemon and lime juices, and sugar and whisk until the sugar is fully dissolved. Add the buttermilk and whisk to combine. Cover the bowl and chill the mixture in the refrigerator for at least 3–4 hours, or overnight, if desired, until it is cold.

3 If you are using an ice cream maker, transfer the mixture to the frozen insert of your ice cream maker and process according to the directions for about 30–60 minutes, or until firm. Transfer to a freezer-proof container, cover, and store in the freezer. Alternatively, pour the mixture into a freezer-proof container, cover with plastic wrap, and freeze for about 2 hours, or until it has begun to harden around the edges. Beat until smooth to get rid of any ice crystals. Freeze again, repeat the process twice, then freeze until it is completely firm.

4 Serve straight from the freezer.

Fruit Cocktail Pops

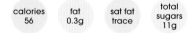

| calories 56 | fat 0.3g | sat fat trace | total sugars 11g | carbs 14g |

INGREDIENTS
makes 8

8 ounces strawberries, hulled
2 small ripe peaches, peeled, pitted, and coarsely chopped (or 2 cups drained canned peaches)
4 large kiwis, peeled and coarsely chopped

sugar syrup

2 tablespoons superfine sugar
5 tablespoons water

METHOD

1 To make the sugar syrup, put the sugar and water into a saucepan over low heat and stir until the sugar has dissolved. Increase the heat until boiling, then simmer for 3–4 minutes. Remove the pan from the heat and let the sugar syrup cool completely before using.

2 Put the strawberries in a blender and process until pureed. Stir in 2 tablespoons of the sugar syrup. Pour the mixture into eight ½-cup ice pop molds. Freeze for 2 hours, or until firm.

3 When the strawberry mixture is frozen, put the peaches in the blender and process until pureed. Stir in half of the remaining sugar syrup. Pour the peach mixture over the frozen strawberry mixture. Insert the ice pop sticks and freeze for 2 hours, or until firm.

4 When the peach mixture is frozen, put the kiwis in the blender and process until pureed. Stir in the remaining sugar syrup. Pour the kiwi mixture over the frozen peach mixture and freeze for 2 hours, or until firm.

5 To unmold the ice pops, dip the frozen molds into warm water for a few seconds and gently release the pops while holding the sticks.

Frozen Hot Chocolate with Hazelnut Liqueur

 calories 242

 fat 8.7g

sat fat 4.9g

 total sugars 23g

carbs 35g

INGREDIENTS
makes 4

3 ounces semisweet chocolate, chopped
2 tablespoons sugar
1 tablespoon unsweetened cocoa powder
1½ cups skim milk
4 cups ice cubes
1 medium banana
¼ cup hazelnut liqueur

METHOD

1 Put the chocolate in the top of a double boiler set over simmering water, or use a heatproof bowl set over a saucepan of gently simmering water, and heat, stirring frequently, until the chocolate has melted.

2 Add the sugar and cocoa powder and heat, stirring constantly, until the sugar has completely dissolved. Remove from the heat and slowly add the milk, stirring until combined. Let cool to room temperature.

3 Transfer the chocolate mixture to a blender and add the ice, banana, and hazelnut liqueur. Blend until well combined and frothy. Pour into 4 cups and serve immediately.

Maple Ice Cream with Nut-Crunch Topping

 calories 193 fat 3.2g sat fat 0.6g total sugars 30g carbs 35.7g

INGREDIENTS

serves 6

ice cream

2 cups 1% milk
1 cup low-fat (2%)
    evaporated milk
¾ cup maple syrup
½ teaspoon maple extract

topping

1 teaspoon unsalted butter
1 tablespoon packed light
    brown sugar
¾ cup corn flakes cereal,
    crushed
2 tablespoons pecan pieces

METHOD

1 If you are using an ice cream maker, freeze the insert of your ice cream maker for at least 24 hours.

2 In a medium bowl, combine the milks, maple syrup, and maple extract and stir to combine well. Cover and chill in the refrigerator for 3 hours (or longer), or until cold.

3 If you are using an ice cream maker, transfer the mixture to the freezer insert of your ice cream maker and process according to the manufacturer's directions for about 30–60 minutes, or until firm. Transfer to a freezer-proof container, cover, and store in the freezer. Alternatively, pour the mixture into a freezer-proof container, cover with plastic wrap, and freeze for about 2 hours, or until it has begun to harden around the edges. Beat until smooth to get rid of any ice crystals. Freeze again, repeat the process twice, then freeze until it is completely firm.

4 To make the topping, cover a baking sheet with parchment paper. Melt the butter in a small saucepan over medium heat. Add the brown sugar and stir to combine. Remove the pan from the heat and add the cereal flakes and pecan pieces, stirring to coat. Transfer the mixture to the prepared baking sheet and let cool to room temperature.

5 Serve the ice cream straight from the freezer and sprinkle with the nut-crunch topping.

Mini Clementine Sorbets

calories 73   fat trace   sat fat trace   total sugars 16g   carbs 19g

INGREDIENTS
makes 10
10 clementines
⅓ cup granulated sugar
¼ cup water
finely grated rind and juice of
   1 lemon
juice of 1 large orange

METHOD

1 Cut a thin slice off the top of each clementine and set aside. Squeeze a little of the juice from each fruit into a blender. Using a teaspoon, scoop the flesh into the blender, then process to a puree.

2 Press the puree through a strainer into a large loaf pan. Put the 10 clementine shells into a roasting pan and freeze to make cups.

3 Put the sugar and water into a heavy saucepan. Heat gently for 5 minutes, or until the sugar has dissolved, tilting the pan to mix them together. Increase the heat and boil rapidly without stirring for 1 minute. Remove from the heat, then stir in the lemon rind and juice. Pour the lemon syrup and orange juice through a strainer and onto the clementine puree, stir, then let cool.

4 Transfer the loaf pan to the freezer and freeze for 2 hours, or until the mixture is semifrozen. Break up the ice crystals using a fork, then return to the freezer for 1 hour. Beat again with the fork, then freeze for an additional 1 hour. Beat again until it resembles colored snow.

5 Spoon the sorbet into the clementine cups, add the lids at a slanted angle, and freeze overnight. (If the sorbet has frozen too firmly, let it soften at room temperature for a few minutes, then beat with a fork.) When ready to serve, transfer the iced desserts to a plate.

Sorbet Sandwiches

calories 154   fat 2.2g   sat fat 1.1g   total sugars 25.5g   carbs 32.6g

INGREDIENTS
makes 8
sorbet
⅔ cup granulated sugar
1⅓ cups water
finely grated rind of 2 limes
¾ cup lime juice
(from about 8 limes)

cookies
¼ cup all-purpose flour,
    plus extra for dusting
¼ cup whole-wheat flour
¼ teaspoon baking soda
⅛ teaspoon salt
¾ teaspoon ground ginger
¼ teaspoon ground cinnamon
pinch of ground cloves
1 tablespoon unsalted butter
2 tablespoons granulated sugar
2 tablespoons dark brown sugar
1 egg
1½ tablespoons unsulfured
    molasses

METHOD
1 To make the sorbet, combine the sugar and ⅔ cup of the water in a small saucepan and bring to a boil. Reduce the heat to a simmer and cook, stirring, for about 2 minutes, or until the sugar has fully dissolved. In a medium bowl, combine the sugar syrup with the remaining ⅔ cup water, and the lime rind and juice. Chill in the refrigerator for about 3 hours (or longer), until cold.

2 Pour the mixture into the chilled insert of an ice cream machine. Churn and freeze according to the manufacturer's directions. Alternatively, pour the mixture into a shallow, freezer-proof container, cover with plastic wrap, and freeze for about 2 hours, until beginning to harden around the edges. Beat until smooth to get rid of any ice crystals. Freeze again, repeat the process twice, then freeze until completely firm.

3 To make the cookies, preheat the oven to 350°F. Line a cookie sheet with parchment paper. In a medium bowl, combine the flours, baking soda, salt, ginger, cinnamon, and cloves. In a large bowl, cream together the butter and the white and brown sugars until light and fluffy. Add the eggs and molasses and mix until incorporated. Add the dry ingredients to the butter mixture and beat on medium speed, scraping down the sides of the bowl once or twice, until incorporated. Refrigerate the dough for about 15 minutes.

4 Lightly dust the work surface with flour and form the dough into 16 balls, about 1½ inches in diameter. Flatten the balls into circles about 3 inches across and ⅛ inch thick and place them a few inches apart on the prepared cookie sheet. Bake in the preheated oven for about 12–14 minutes, or until the cookies are beginning to crisp. Remove from the oven and transfer the cookies to a wire rack to cool completely.

5 To make the sandwiches, place a scoop of the frozen sorbet onto the flat side of a cookie, then press another cookie on top. Scrape off any sorbet that squeezes out the sides into the sorbet container. Repeat until you have eight sandwiches. Wrap the sandwiches individually in parchment paper or plastic wrap and store in the freezer. Remove from the freezer about 15 minutes before serving.

Like a Big
Warm Hug!

Chewy Chocolate Cookies

calories 79	fat 3.2g	sat fat 1.9g	total sugars 7.5g	carbs 12g

INGREDIENTS
makes 30

1¼ cups all-purpose flour, plus extra for dusting

¼ cup unsweetened cocoa powder

¼ teaspoon baking soda

¼ teaspoon salt

1 cup granulated sugar

6 tablespoons unsalted butter, softened

3 egg whites

1 teaspoon vanilla extract

¼ cup semisweet chocolate chips

METHOD

1 Preheat the oven to 350°F. Line a cookie sheet with parchment paper.

2 In a medium bowl, combine the flour, cocoa powder, baking soda, and salt.

3 In a large bowl, use an electric mixer to cream together the sugar and butter until fluffy. Add the egg whites, vanilla extract, and chocolate chips and mix until well combined.

4 Lightly flour your hands and form rounded tablespoons of dough into balls. Put these onto the prepared cookie sheet, setting them about 2 inches apart. Bake in the preheated oven for 10–12 minutes, or until set.

5 Transfer the cookies to a wire rack to cool completely before serving.

Raisin Apple Turnovers

| calories 130 | fat 1.1g | sat fat trace | total sugars 11.7g | carbs 27.4g |

INGREDIENTS
makes 6

cooking spray
1 Granny Smith apple, peeled, cored, and diced
2 tablespoons raisins
2 tablespoons light brown sugar
6 sheets frozen phyllo dough, thawed

METHOD

1 Preheat the oven to 375°F. Spray a baking sheet with cooking spray.

2 To make the filling, place the apples, raisins, and brown sugar in a large bowl and toss to mix well.

3 To make the turnovers, lay one sheet of phyllo on your work surface and spritz all over with cooking spray. Lay the second phyllo sheet on top and spritz that one all over with cooking spray. Lay the third sheet on top. Using kitchen scissors, cut the stack lengthwise into three long strips.

4 Place a heaping tablespoon of the filling at one end of one of the strips, leaving about 2 inches at the end. Fold the uncovered end over the filling at a 45-degree angle. Continue folding end over end to form a triangular, fully enclosed bundle. Repeat with the other two strips and set the triangles on a baking sheet. Repeat the entire process with the remaining three sheets of phyllo and the rest of the filling.

5 Spray the turnovers lightly with cooking spray. Bake in the preheated oven for about 15 minutes, or until the turnovers are lightly browned and crisp. Serve warm or at room temperature.

Vanilla Soufflé Omelets

 calories 163

 fat 8g

sat fat 4.5g

total sugars 8.5g

 carbs 12g

INGREDIENTS
serves 4

8 egg whites
2 tablespoons honey,
   plus extra for drizzling
1½ teaspoons cornstarch
2 teaspoons vanilla extract
1 cup ricotta cheese
sunflower oil, for brushing
1⅔ cups raspberries

METHOD

1 Whisk the egg whites in a large, grease-free bowl until they form soft peaks.

2 Add the honey, cornstarch, and vanilla and whisk to mix evenly. Beat the ricotta in a small bowl until smooth, then fold lightly into the egg white mixture.

3 Brush a large, heavy skillet with oil and put over medium heat. Spoon one-quarter of the egg white mixture into the skillet and spread evenly with a spatula.

4 Cook for 3–4 minutes, or until golden brown underneath. Turn the omelet over and cook for 2–3 minutes on the other side, then sprinkle with one-quarter of the raspberries. Gently lift one side with the spatula and fold the omelet in half to enclose.

5 Cook for an additional few seconds, then flip over onto a serving plate. Keep warm and repeat with the remaining mixture to make a total of four omelets. Serve immediately, drizzled with honey to taste.

Lemon-Glazed Gingerbread Cake

 calories 237   fat 10.9g   sat fat 1g total sugars 17g carbs 32.8g

INGREDIENTS
serves 16
cooking spray
1¼ cups all-purpose flour
1¼ cups whole-wheat flour
1 tablespoon ground ginger
1½ teaspoons ground
    cinnamon
1 teaspoon salt
1 teaspoon baking powder
½ teaspoon baking soda
⅔ cup molasses
⅔ cup hot water
½ cup firmly packed light
    brown sugar
½ cup canola oil
⅓ cup unsweetened
    applesauce
2 eggs, beaten

glaze
¾ cup confectioners' sugar
3 tablespoons lemon juice
1 tablespoon finely grated
    lemon rind

METHOD
1 Preheat the oven to 350°F. Spray a 10-inch Bundt cake pan with cooking spray.

2 In a medium bowl, whisk together the flours, ginger, cinnamon, salt, baking powder, and baking soda. Put the molasses in a large heatproof bowl and pour the hot water over it, then mix until blended. Mix in the brown sugar, canola oil, applesauce, and eggs until combined. Slowly add the flour mixture, beating until combined.

3 Transfer the batter to the prepared Bundt pan and bake in the preheated oven for about 30 minutes, or until a toothpick inserted into the center comes out clean. Remove from the oven and let cool for about 15 minutes, then turn it out onto a wire rack and let cool completely.

4 To make the glaze, stir together the confectioners' sugar, lemon juice, and rind until smooth. Drizzle the glaze over the cooled cake. Slice the cake into wedges and serve at room temperature.

Salted Caramel Bread Pudding

 calories 247

 fat 5g

sat fat 2g

 total sugars 28g

carbs 43g

INGREDIENTS

serves 8

cooking spray
8 slices whole-wheat bread,
    cut into cubes
1 cup fat-free evaporated milk
¾ cup 1% milk
2 eggs
⅓ cup maple syrup
1 teaspoon vanilla extract
½ teaspoon ground cinnamon
1 Granny Smith apple, cored
    and cut into ½-inch cubes

sauce

1 tablespoon unsalted butter
½ cup firmly packed light
    brown sugar
1 tablespoon bourbon or
    other whiskey
⅓ cup whole milk
pinch of salt
¾ teaspoon vanilla extract

METHOD

1 Preheat the oven to 350°F. Spray an 8-inch square baking dish with cooking spray.

2 Put the bread cubes on a baking sheet and bake in the preheated oven for about 6–8 minutes, or until they just begin to brown. Leave the oven on.

3 In a large bowl, whisk together both types of milk, the eggs, maple syrup, vanilla extract, and cinnamon. Add the apple cubes and bread. Let the mixture stand, stirring occasionally, until the bread soaks up the liquid.

4 To make the sauce, combine the butter, brown sugar, and bourbon in a small saucepan over medium–high heat and cook, swirling the pan, until the sugar has dissolved. Add the milk and the salt and bring to a boil. Boil for about an additional 5 minutes, until the mixture thickens. Remove from the heat and stir in the vanilla extract.

5 Transfer the bread mixture to the prepared baking dish, drizzle the sauce over the top, and bake in the preheated oven for about 45 minutes, or until it puffs up and begins to brown around the edges. Serve immediately.

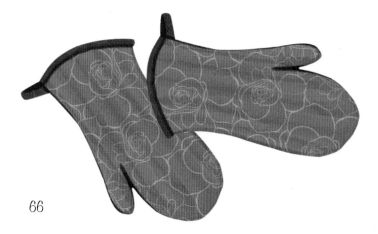

Apple-Berry Crisp

 calories 237 fat 7g sat fat 4g total sugars 38g carbs 48g

INGREDIENTS
serves 8
cooking spray
6 Pippin or other crisp apples,
    peeled, cored, and sliced
½ cup dried cranberries
    or dried cherries
¼ cup granulated sugar
½ teaspoon vanilla extract

topping
½ cup all-purpose flour
½ cup firmly packed light
    brown sugar
½ teaspoon ground cinnamon
pinch of salt
4 tablespoons butter, at room
    temperature
½ cup rolled oats

METHOD
1 Preheat the oven to 375°F. Spray a baking dish with cooking spray.

2 To make the filling, put the apples, dried fruit, sugar, and vanilla extract into a medium bowl and toss to mix thoroughly. Spread the mixture in the prepared baking dish, overlapping the apples a little as necessary.

3 To make the topping, combine the flour, brown sugar, cinnamon, and salt in the bowl of a food processor or in a large mixing bowl. In the processor, or using a pastry cutter or two knives, cut the butter into the flour mixture until it resembles coarse bread crumbs. Stir in the oats.

4 Sprinkle the topping evenly over the filling and bake in the preheated oven for about 45 minutes, or until the topping is crisp and beginning to brown. Serve immediately.

Maple-Peach Quinoa Pudding

 calories 180   fat 3.2g   sat fat 0.8g   total sugars 20.5g   carbs 31g

INGREDIENTS
serves 6

cooking spray
⅓ cup quinoa
2 cups water
2 cups skim milk
2 eggs
¼ cup maple syrup
¼ cup unsweetened
    applesauce
2 cups peeled, diced peaches
2 tablespoons packed light
    brown sugar

METHOD

1 Preheat the oven to 350°F. Spray six ¾-cup ramekins (individual ceramic dishes) with cooking spray.

2 In a small saucepan, combine the quinoa with the water and bring to a boil. Reduce the heat to low, cover, and simmer for about 15 minutes, or until the quinoa is tender. Drain well in a fine-meshed strainer.

3 In a medium bowl, whisk together the milk, eggs, maple syrup, and applesauce until well combined. Stir in the quinoa and divide the mixture among the prepared ramekins. Bake in the preheated oven for about 35–40 minutes, or until completely set.

4 Spray a nonstick skillet with cooking spray and heat it over medium heat. Add the diced peaches and cook, stirring frequently, until heated through. Remove the pan from the heat and sprinkle the brown sugar over the peaches. Stir until the sugar melts and coats the peaches evenly. Set aside to cool.

5 Spoon the peaches equally over the puddings. Serve warm or at room temperature.

Pumpkin Custard with Whipped Cinnamon Topping

| calories 232 | fat 4.4g | sat fat 1.4g | total sugars 30.7g | carbs 37.6g |

INGREDIENTS

serves 4

custard

cooking spray
3 eggs, beaten
1 cup canned pumpkin puree
⅓ cup firmly packed light
    brown sugar
½ cup skim milk
1 tablespoon all-purpose flour
2 teaspoons vanilla extract
¼ teaspoon ground cinnamon
pinch of nutmeg
pinch of salt

topping

1 egg white
2 tablespoons granulated sugar
¼ teaspoon cream of tartar
¼ cup low-fat evaporated milk,
    chilled
½ teaspoon vanilla extract
⅛ teaspoon ground cinnamon

METHOD

1 Preheat the oven to 350°F. Spray four ¾-cup ramekins (individual ceramic dishes) with cooking spray.

2 In a medium bowl, combine the eggs, pumpkin puree, brown sugar, milk, flour, vanilla extract, cinnamon, nutmeg, and salt. Mix well. Spoon the custard into the prepared ramekins, dividing it equally. Place the filled ramekins in a baking dish and pour boiling water into the dish so that it comes about halfway up the sides of the ramekins. Bake in the preheated oven for about 35 minutes, until the custard is set. Transfer to a wire rack to cool.

3 To make the topping, put the egg white and sugar into a bowl set over a saucepan of simmering water and whisk until the mixture is warm to the touch and the sugar is completely dissolved. Add the cream of tartar and beat with an electric mixer fitted with a whisk attachment until stiff peaks form. Add the evaporated milk, vanilla extract, and cinnamon and whisk until the mixture holds soft peaks.

4 Serve the custards in the ramekins either warm or at room temperature, topped with a spoonful of the whipped topping.

Go For It!

Are you a guilt-free girl who hates to exercise? Would you rather spend an afternoon at the dentist than go to the gym? Well, guess what? Even if you hate exercising with a fiery passion (or you are just too lazy or busy to make it to the gym on a regular basis), don't worry. You can be healthy without spending all your free time working out. Work more activity into your day, every day, and you'll be well on your way to a healthy body (and appetite)!

Getting more exercise while you go about your normal life is easy. You have to cook, clean up, do laundry, and so forth anyway, so you might as well get credit for it, right? Here are how many calories the average person burns while doing everyday activities:

Grocery shopping (60 minutes): **150**

Ironing (10 minutes): **25**

Cooking (60 minutes): **85**

Washing dishes (60 minutes): **75**

Putting away groceries (10 minutes): **30**

Cleaning the house (60 minutes): **150**

Gardening (60 minutes): **240**

Even better, you can even use exercise as an excuse to have more fun, such as, say, more time spent shopping for shoes or gossiping with your girlfriends. Here's how many calories the average woman burns in 60 minutes of some of the more enjoyable activities:

Taking a leisurely walk to enjoy the spring flowers or stop and get a frothy skinny cappuccino: **200**

Shopping for the perfect pair of strappy heels or knee-high boots: **150**

Getting the latest gossip from your friends (while taking a brisk walk, of course): **300**

Shaking it on the dance floor: **400**

So if you really want to burn some calories, you could spend the day cleaning your house or working in the yard. Better yet, walk with a girlfriend to get your caffeine fix, then head to the mall for a good three-hour shopping expedition (in which you could easily burn more than 650 calories!), head out to a dance club with your honey, and spend an hour getting down on the dance floor.

You will have easily earned yourself any of the desserts in this book, and maybe even two servings!

Pistachio Angel Cake

calories
170

fat
3g

sat fat
0.3g

total
sugars
22g

carbs
32g

INGREDIENTS

serves 8

sunflower oil, for greasing
6 egg whites
¾ teaspoon cream of tartar
¾ cup granulated sugar
1 teaspoon vanilla extract
⅓ cup finely chopped
    pistachio nuts
½ cup rice flour, plus extra
    for dusting
fresh fruit, to serve

METHOD

1 Preheat the oven to 325°F. Grease a 1½-quart tube pan and dust lightly with a little flour, tipping out the excess.

2 Whisk the egg whites with an electric mixer in a large, grease-free bowl until they hold soft peaks. Stir the cream of tartar into the sugar in a small bowl, then gradually whisk into the egg whites, beating at high speed until the mixture holds stiff peaks. Beat in the vanilla extract.

3 In a separate small bowl, stir the pistachios into the flour. Fold the pistachio mixture into the egg white mixture lightly and evenly, using a large metal spoon.

4 Spoon the batter into the prepared pan and tap the pan to remove any large air bubbles. Bake in the preheated oven for 25–30 minutes, or until golden brown and firm to the touch.

5 Turn out the cake onto a wire rack and let cool, upside down, in the pan. When cool, run the tip of a knife around the edges of the cake to loosen, then turn out onto a plate and serve with fresh fruit.

Almond Cupcakes with Poached Pears

 calories 217 fat 4.2g sat fat 1.5g total sugars 32.6g carbs 43g

INGREDIENTS
makes 12
6 cups water
1 cup granulated sugar
6 small pears, halved, peeled, and cored
1 cinnamon stick

topping
1 egg white
2 tablespoons granulated sugar
¼ teaspoon cream of tartar
¼ cup low-fat evaporated milk, chilled
½ teaspoon vanilla extract
½ teaspoon ground cinnamon

almond cupcakes
cooking spray
⅓ cup ground almonds (almond meal)
⅓ cup all-purpose flour
½ teaspoon baking powder
⅛ teaspoon salt
2 tablespoons unsalted butter
½ cup superfine sugar
1 teaspoon vanilla extract or almond extract
1 egg

METHOD

1 To make the poached pears, put the water and the sugar into a large saucepan and bring to a boil. Reduce the heat to a simmer and cook, stirring, until the sugar has dissolved. Add the pears and cinnamon stick and simmer gently for about 20 minutes, until the pears are tender. Drain the pears, discarding the cooking liquid, and set aside.

2 To make the topping, put the egg white and sugar in the top of a double boiler set over simmering water, or use a heatproof bowl set over a saucepan of simmering water, and whisk until the sugar has completely dissolved. Add the cream of tartar and whisk with an electric mixer for about 3 minutes, or until stiff peaks form. Add the evaporated milk, vanilla extract, and cinnamon and whisk until the mixture holds soft peaks. Chill until ready to serve.

3 To make the almond cupcakes, preheat the oven to 350°F. Spray a mini muffin pan with cooking spray. Combine the ground almonds, flour, baking powder, and salt in a medium bowl. In a large bowl, cream together the butter and sugar with an electric mixer until light and fluffy. Add the vanilla extract and the egg and beat on medium–high speed until combined. Add half of the flour mixture and beat on medium–high speed until incorporated. Add the remaining flour and beat until incorporated.

4 Spoon the batter into the prepared muffin pan, filling each cup about one-third full. Bake in the preheated oven for 13–14 minutes, or until the cupcakes just begin to brown around the edges. Remove the cupcakes from the pan and serve warm with half a poached pear and a spoonful of whipped topping.

Fresh, Fruity & Fabulous!

Berry & Rhubarb Cheesecake Bars

 calories 149   fat 4g   sat fat 1.5g   total sugars 16.3g   carbs 22.3g

INGREDIENTS
makes 8

cooking spray
10 graham crackers
1 tablespoon packed light brown sugar
1 tablespoon unsalted butter, melted
1 teaspoon water
1 cup fresh mixed berries (blackberries, blueberries, strawberries, or raspberries, diced if large)
1 cup diced fresh rhubarb

filling

1 cup fat-free cream cheese
¼ cup honey
2 eggs, lightly beaten
1 teaspoon vanilla extract
1 teaspoon grated lemon rind

METHOD

1 Preheat the oven to 350°F. Spray an 8-inch square baking pan with cooking spray.

2 Pulse the graham crackers and brown sugar in a food processor until coarsely ground. Add the melted butter and the water and process until the mixture is moist. Press the mixture into the prepared pan in an even layer. Bake the crust in the preheated oven for about 10–12 minutes, or until it begins to brown. Remove from the oven, leaving the oven on, and let cool while you prepare the filling.

3 To make the filling, beat together the cream cheese and honey with an electric mixer until smooth. Add the eggs, vanilla extract, and lemon rind and beat until fluffy.

4 Spread the cream cheese mixture on top of the cooled crust in an even layer. Sprinkle the berries and rhubarb evenly over the top. Bake in the preheated oven for about 30 minutes, or until the filling is mostly set. Remove from the oven and let cool to room temperature, then refrigerate to chill completely for about 2 hours.

5 Slice into 8 bars and serve chilled.

Broiled Fruit Kabobs

calories 164   **fat** 8g   **sat fat** 0.5g   **total sugars** 22g   **carbs** 22g

INGREDIENTS
serves 4

2 tablespoons hazelnut oil
2 tablespoons honey
juice and grated rind of 1 lime
2 pineapple slices,
    cut into chunks
8 strawberries
1 pear, cored and
    thickly sliced
1 banana, thickly sliced
2 kiwis, quartered

METHOD

1 Preheat the broiler to medium. Mix together the oil, honey, and lime juice and rind in a large, shallow dish. Add the fruit and turn to coat. Cover and let marinate for 10 minutes.

2 Thread the fruit onto four metal skewers, beginning with a pineapple piece and ending with a strawberry.

3 Brush the kabobs with the marinade and cook under the preheated broiler, brushing frequently with the marinade, for 5 minutes. Turn the kabobs over, brush with the remaining marinade, and broil for an additional 5 minutes. Serve immediately.

Port-Roasted Cherries with Vanilla Bean Topping

| calories 137 | fat trace | sat fat trace | total sugars 26.2g | carbs 28.2g |

INGREDIENTS
serves 4
port-roasted cherries
2 cups pitted, ripe fresh cherries
2 tablespoons granulated sugar
¼ cup ruby port

topping
1 egg white
2 tablespoons granulated sugar
¼ teaspoon cream of tartar
¼ cup low-fat evaporated milk, chilled
½ teaspoon vanilla extract
1 vanilla bean

METHOD

1 Preheat the oven to 450°F.

2 Put the cherries in a baking dish and sprinkle the sugar over them. Roast in the preheated oven for about 10 minutes, or until the cherries soften and juice begins to leak out. Remove the dish from the oven and pour the port over the cherries, stirring to coat the cherries and deglaze the pan. Return the dish to the oven for another 5 minutes, or until the liquid begins to bubble and thicken.

3 To make the topping, put the egg white and sugar in the top of a double boiler set over simmering water, or use a heatproof bowl set over a saucepan of gently simmering water, and whisk until the mixture is warm to the touch and the sugar has completely dissolved. Add the cream of tartar and beat with an electric mixer until stiff peaks form. Add the evaporated milk and vanilla extract. Using a sharp knife, split the vanilla bean lengthwise and scrape the seeds into the egg white mixture. Beat for an additional 3 minutes, or until the mixture holds soft peaks.

4 Serve the cherries warm in dessert glasses or martini glasses, topped with a spoonful of the whipped topping.

Fig & Watermelon Salad

 calories 196
 fat 1g
sat fat 0.5g
 total sugars 44g
carbs 43g

INGREDIENTS
serves 4
⅓ watermelon
   (about 3¼ pounds)
¾ cup seedless black grapes
4 figs

syrup dressing
1 lime
grated rind and juice of
   1 orange
1 tablespoon maple syrup
2 tablespoons honey

METHOD

1 Cut the watermelon into wedges and scoop out and discard the seeds. Cut the flesh away from the rind, then chop the flesh into 1-inch cubes. Put the watermelon cubes in a bowl with the grapes. Cut each fig lengthwise into eight wedges and add to the bowl.

2 Grate the lime and mix the rind with the orange rind and juice, maple syrup, and honey in a small saucepan. Bring to a boil over low heat. Pour the mixture over the fruit and stir. Let cool. Stir again, cover, and chill in the refrigerator for at least 1 hour, stirring occasionally.

3 Divide the fruit salad equally among four bowls and serve.

Broiled Stone Fruit

 calories 172   fat 5.4g sat fat 2.1g   total sugars 21.2g carbs 27g

INGREDIENTS
serves 6

1½ cups low-fat ricotta cheese

2 teaspoons freshly grated
    orange rind

3 firm, ripe peaches, pitted and
    quartered

3 firm, ripe nectarines,
    pitted and quartered

3 ripe plums, apricots, or figs,
    pitted and halved or
    quartered

2 tablespoons orange blossom
    honey

2 tablespoons slivered almonds

METHOD

1 In a medium bowl, stir together the ricotta and orange rind.

2 Preheat the broiler to medium–high and broil the fruit, cut side down, turning once or twice, for about 5 minutes, or until they are softened and beginning to caramelize.

3 To serve, spoon the ricotta into six small dessert bowls or custard cups. Top each with some broiled fruit, drizzle with the honey, and sprinkle the almonds over the top. Serve immediately.

91

What's on the guilt-free dessert menu?

Living the guilt-free lifestyle helps you to think about what you are eating and to plan ahead so you always have delicious, but healthy, snacks at your fingertips. It is a good idea to keep some sweet treats in the pantry as a standby. Why not make a batch of our Caramel Popcorn Bites as these small treats can satisfy hunger pangs between meals? Don't wait until you are starving before choosing your snack. That's how you end up making bad choices—trust us, we know!

Before you go grocery shopping, make a list. Include healthy ingredients, such as raspberries, peaches, apples, and so on, on the list. Make sure to list plenty of healthy, sweet snacks—yogurts, dried fruits, smoothies, frozen yogurt. If you've got a refrigerator full of fresh, healthy ingredients, you'll be more tempted to reach for a piece of fruit or yogurt when hungry.

Dice up any large fruits, such as melons or pineapples, so that they'll be an inviting, easy, and appetizing snack. It's also easy to freeze batches of diced fruit so you can buy and prepare these snacks in advance and have them on standby!

Of course, your life wouldn't be worth living if you couldn't eat out now and then, too. And rest assured, you can!

Again, planning ahead can make a big difference. Check out the restaurant's menu online before you go and decide which dessert you'll order. Steer away from anything with ice cream, heavy cream, or pastry, and opt for lighter dishes, such as sorbets or baked fruits.

And when you just want something sweet and deliciously satisfying, look no farther than the pages in this book. Indulge your cravings with surprisingly light Spiced Strawberry Meringue Soufflé; Broiled Stone Fruit with ricotta, honey, and almonds; or our creamy tasting, but light Orange Yogurt Panna Cotta. These recipes all taste amazing and are totally guilt free!

Spiced Strawberry Meringue Soufflé

| calories 157 | fat 0.3g | sat fat trace | total sugars 32.6g | carbs 37.5g |

INGREDIENTS
serves 6

4 cups diced fresh strawberries
⅓ cup granulated sugar
¼ cup water
1 tablespoon cornstarch
1 teaspoon vanilla extract
½ teaspoon pepper

topping

3 egg whites
½ cup superfine sugar
¼ teaspoon cream of tartar

METHOD

1 Preheat the oven to 400°F. Put the strawberries, sugar, and water in a saucepan and bring to a simmer over medium heat, stirring frequently. In a small bowl, combine the cornstarch with 1 tablespoon of water and stir to combine. Add the cornstarch mixture to the simmering strawberry mixture and cook, stirring, for about 1 minute, or until thickened. Stir in the vanilla extract and pepper and remove from the heat. Set aside to cool.

2 In a large bowl, whisk the egg whites with an electric mixer on medium–high speed until they form soft peaks. Gradually add the sugar and the cream of tartar and continue to whisk on medium–high speed until stiff, glossy peaks form. Scoop about ⅓ cup of the strawberry mixture from the saucepan and, using a spoon or a rubber spatula, swirl it into the meringue with just a few stirs.

3 Spoon the remaining strawberry mixture into six ¾-cup ramekins (individual ceramic dishes) and set the ramekins on a baking sheet. Top with the meringue mixture, mounding it up and using a fingertip to swirl it into peaks.

4 Place the baking sheet in the preheated oven and bake for 5–6 minutes, or until the peaks begin to turn golden brown. Serve warm.

Peach Popovers

 calories 167
 fat 3g
sat fat 1g
 total sugars 11g
carbs 31g

INGREDIENTS
serves 4

1 teaspoon sunflower oil,
    plus extra for greasing
¾ cup all-purpose flour
1 extra-large egg white
1 cup low-fat milk
1 teaspoon vanilla extract
3 peaches, sliced
maple syrup, to serve

METHOD

1 Preheat the oven to 400°F. Grease 12 cups in a muffin pan.

2 Put the oil, flour, egg white, milk, and vanilla extract·in a large bowl. Beat thoroughly to a smooth, bubbly batter.

3 Put the prepared muffin pan in the preheated oven for 5 minutes. Remove the pan from the oven and quickly divide the peach slices among the cups of the pan and pour the batter evenly into each cup.

4 Bake the popovers for 15–20 minutes, or until well risen, crisp, and golden brown.

5 Remove the popovers carefully from the pan with a small spatula. Serve immediately with maple syrup.

Orange Yogurt Panna Cotta

calories 235	fat 1.2g	sat fat 0.6g	total sugars 49g	carbs 52g

INGREDIENTS
makes 6

3 tablespoons freshly squeezed orange juice
2 teaspoons powdered gelatin
2 cups low-fat milk
1½ cups low-fat plain yogurt
⅓ cup honey
1 teaspoon vanilla extract
2 teaspoons grated orange rind

compote

1¾ cups fresh or frozen blackberries
¼ cup water
¼ cup granulated sugar
2 tablespoons lemon juice

METHOD

1 To make the panna cotta, pour the orange juice into a small bowl and sprinkle the gelatin over the top. Set aside until the gelatin has absorbed the liquid.

2 In a medium saucepan, combine the milk, yogurt, honey, and vanilla extract, set the pan over medium–high heat, and bring to a simmer (do not boil), stirring to incorporate the yogurt and honey. Remove from the heat, then stir in the orange rind and the moistened gelatin mixture. Whisk until the gelatin is fully dissolved. Ladle the mixture into six ¾-cup ramekins (individual ceramic dishes), dividing it equally. Let cool to room temperature, then cover loosely and refrigerate for at least 4 hours, or until set.

3 To make the compote, combine the blackberries, water, sugar, and lemon juice in a medium saucepan and set over medium–high heat. Bring to a boil, then reduce heat to medium–low and simmer until the sugar has dissolved, the liquid begins to thicken, and the fruit begins to break down. Remove from heat and let cool to room temperature.

4 Serve the panna cotta chilled in the ramekins, with the compote spooned over the top.

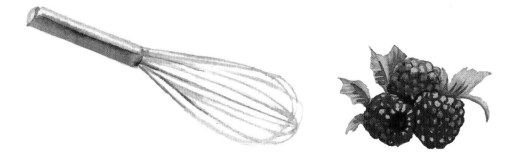

Fluffy Lemon Whips

 calories 77 | fat 0.8g | sat fat 0.5g | total sugars 12g | carbs 13g

INGREDIENTS
serves 4

2 tablespoons lemon juice
3 tablespoons agave syrup
    or honey
1 mint sprig, plus extra
    to decorate
2 egg whites
1 teaspoon finely grated
    lemon rind
⅔ cup low-fat Greek-style yogurt

METHOD

1 Put the lemon juice, syrup, and mint sprig in a small saucepan over high heat and bring to a boil, stirring. Remove from the heat and let stand for 10 minutes.

2 Meanwhile, put the egg whites in a large, grease-free bowl and beat with an electric mixer until they hold stiff peaks.

3 Remove the mint from the syrup. Add the lemon rind to the syrup and then gradually drizzle the syrup into the egg whites, beating at high speed, until soft peaks form.

4 Add the yogurt to the egg white mixture and fold in lightly with a large metal spoon.

5 Spoon the mixture into four tall glasses or individual dishes and top each with a mint sprig. Serve immediately.

Stuffed Nectarines

calories 93 **fat 0.2g** **sat fat trace** **total sugars 20g** **carbs 16g**

INGREDIENTS
serves 4

4 ripe, firm nectarines
    or peaches
1¼ cups blueberries
1 cup raspberries
⅔ cup freshly squeezed
    orange juice
1–2 teaspoons honey,
    or to taste
1 tablespoon brandy (optional)
¼ cup fat-free Greek yogurt
1 tablespoon finely grated
    orange rind

METHOD

1 Preheat the oven to 350°F. Cut the nectarines in half, remove the pits, then put in a shallow ovenproof dish.

2 Mix together the blueberries and raspberries in a bowl and use to fill the hollows left by the removal of the nectarine pits. Spoon any extra berries around the edge.

3 Mix together the orange juice, honey, and brandy, if using, in a small bowl and pour the liquid over the fruit. Blend the yogurt with the grated orange rind in another bowl and let chill in the refrigerator until required.

4 Bake the berry-filled nectarines in the preheated oven for 10 minutes, or until the fruit is hot. Serve immediately with the orange-flavored yogurt.

Dinner Party Showstoppers

Strawberry & White Chocolate Napoleons

calories 249	fat 8g	sat fat 2.7g	total sugars 36g	carbs 50g

INGREDIENTS
makes 8

6 sheets frozen phyllo dough, thawed
cooking spray
1½ teaspoons granulated sugar
2⅓ pints fresh strawberries, sliced
2 tablespoons confectioners' sugar, to decorate

filling

3½ ounces white chocolate, chopped
⅓ cup plus ½ cup water
⅔ cup granulated sugar
3 egg whites
¼ teaspoon cream of tartar

METHOD

1 Preheat the oven to 350°F and cover a large baking sheet with parchment paper.

2 To make the phyllo squares, carefully separate one phyllo sheet from the others, lay it on your work surface, and spritz it all over with the cooking spray. Sprinkle with about ¼ teaspoon of the sugar. Lay another sheet of phyllo over the top of the first one and repeat the steps until you have three layers. Cut the stack of phyllo sheets into 12 squares and transfer to the prepared baking sheet. Repeat with the remaining three sheets of phyllo dough so that you have 24 squares. Bake the phyllo squares in the preheated oven for about 6–8 minutes, until lightly browned. Remove from the oven and let cool completely on the sheet.

3 To make the filling, put the white chocolate and the ⅓ cup of water in the top of a double boiler set over simmering water, or use a heatproof bowl set over a saucepan of gently simmering water. Heat, stirring frequently, until the chocolate has completely melted and the mixture is smooth. Set aside.

4 In a small saucepan, combine the sugar with the remaining ½ cup of water and bring to a boil. Cook, stirring, for about 5 minutes, or until the mixture begins to thicken.

5 Beat the egg whites in large bowl with an electric mixer until foamy. Add the cream of tartar and beat for about an additional 3 minutes, gradually increasing the speed, until soft peaks form. With the mixer running, slowly add the warm sugar mixture to the egg white mixture. Increase the speed to high and beat until the mixture has cooled and stiff, glossy peaks form.

6 Whisk one-third of the egg white mixture into the melted chocolate until it is well combined. Whisk in the remaining egg white mixture. Transfer the mixture to a medium bowl, cover, and chill in the refrigerator for at least an hour.

7 Just before serving, lay eight phyllo squares on your work surface. Top each with about 2 tablespoons of the white chocolate mousse, then top this with four to five strawberry slices and another square of phyllo. Repeat with another layer of mousse and strawberries. Finish with a phyllo square and a dusting of confectioners' sugar. Serve immediately.

Summer Meringue

| calories 110 | fat 4g | sat fat 3g | total sugars 11g | carbs 11g |

INGREDIENTS

serves 6

meringue

2 egg whites
3 tablespoons superfine sugar
1 teaspoon cornstarch
1 teaspoon vanilla extract
1 teaspoon vinegar

filling

1 cup low-fat cream cheese
⅔ cup low-fat plain yogurt
½–1 teaspoon vanilla extract,
 or to taste
2½ cups mixed berries
 (quartered or halved if large)

METHOD

1 Preheat the oven to 250°F and line a baking sheet with parchment paper. To make the meringue, whisk the egg whites in a large, grease-free bowl until stiff, then gradually add the sugar, a spoonful at a time, whisking well after each addition. Stir in the cornstarch, vanilla extract, and vinegar.

2 When all the sugar has been added and the mixture is stiff, spoon onto the lined baking sheet and form into a 6-inch circle, hollowing out the center to form a shell.

3 Bake in the preheated oven for 1½–2 hours, or until crisp. Turn the oven off and let cool in the oven. Remove from the oven and let rest until cold before removing from the baking sheet. Store in an airtight container until required.

4 To make the filling, beat together the cream cheese and yogurt in a bowl until well blended, then stir in the vanilla extract. When ready to serve, pile the cheese filling in the center of the meringue shell, top with the fruits, and serve, cut into six pieces.

Blood Orange Polenta Tart

 calories 205

 fat 2.9g

sat fat 1g

 total sugars 31g

 carbs 40g

INGREDIENTS
serves 8

cooking spray
1 cup cooked polenta or
    cornmeal
¼ cup firmly packed light brown
    sugar, plus 1 tablespoon
3 blood oranges or small
    navel oranges

filling
4 eggs
⅔ cup superfine sugar
⅔ cup orange juice
1 tablespoon lemon juice
½ cup low-fat milk
½ teaspoon vanilla extract
1 teaspoon finely grated
    orange rind

METHOD

1 Preheat the oven to 350°F. Spray a 9-inch springform tart pan with cooking spray.

2 To make the crust, combine the cooked polenta with ¼ cup of the brown sugar in a medium bowl and mix well. Spread the dough into a thin layer in the prepared tart pan and bake in the preheated oven for about 20 minutes, or until it begins to brown.

3 To make the filling, whisk together the eggs, sugar, orange juice, lemon juice, milk, and vanilla extract. Stir in the orange rind, then pour the mixture onto the polenta crust in an even layer. Bake in the preheated oven for about 15 minutes, or until the filling begins to set.

4 While the tart is baking, slice the oranges into thin circles, using a serrated knife. When the filling is partly set, remove the tart from the oven and arrange the orange slices on top. Sprinkle the remaining tablespoon of brown sugar over the top and return the tart to the oven. Bake another 6–8 minutes, or until the filling is mostly set.

5 Remove from the oven and set the pan on a wire rack to cool. Slice the tart into wedges and serve.

Curbing Those Cravings!

No matter how healthy your lifestyle, you're bound to battle unbeatable cravings now and then. As many a failed dieter will tell you, trying to defeat such intense urges through deprivation and sheer will is pointless. Instead, make guilt-free choices that feed your body and soul, without packing on the pounds!

Fresh fruit is always a great choice when you're craving something sweet. Juicy berries, succulent melon, crisp apples, and luscious stone fruits can be surprisingly satisfying. Port-Roasted Cherries with Vanilla Bean Topping are a fantastically healthy and tasty way to add an extra serving of fruit to your day.

Sometimes a sweet sip of something warm is just the thing you need to take the edge off a sugar craving. Honey-sweetened herbal teas, such as cinnamon or raspberry, and hot cocoa made with skim milk can hit the spot on a chilly evening.

If it's a sweltering summer day and all you can think about is a cool, creamy, refreshing ice cream cone, opt for low-fat or fat-free frozen yogurt or sorbet instead. Our Maple Ice Cream with Nut-Crunch Topping, Red Wine Sorbet, or Lemon Buttermilk Sherbet will do the job nicely. And you'll save yourself potentially hundreds of calories and as many as 16 grams of fat. Skip the cone (ask for your scoop in a dish instead) and you'll save another 25 to 100 calories.

Instead of a creamy cheesecake or chocolate pudding, try our Pumpkin Custard with Whipped Cinnamon Topping. This is made with skim milk so contains all of the flavor with much less fat! Or why not try our Frozen Hot Chocolate spiked with hazelnut liqueur, made with skim milk and banana?

If chocolate is what you need, opt for a small serving of dark chocolate. It's lower in fat than milk chocolate, and is packed with antioxidants, healthy nutrients that reduce your risk of high blood pressure, high cholesterol, and heart disease and limit the effects of aging on your cells. Our Chewy Chocolate Cookies deliver a double dose of rich dark chocolate because they're made with both cocoa powder and semisweet chocolate.

Remember the golden rule of a healthy, guilt-free girl's life: It's not about deprivation, but moderation that makes keeping fit and healthy doable and, dare we say, even enjoyable.

Mini Molten Chocolate Cakes

 calories 235

 fat 10.8g

sat fat 4.2g

total sugars 19g

carbs 31g

INGREDIENTS
makes 8

cooking spray
1 tablespoon plus
   1 teaspoon granulated sugar
3 ounces semisweet chocolate,
   chopped
1½ tablespoons unsalted butter,
   cut into chunks
1½ tablespoons whole milk
2½ teaspoons light corn syrup

cake

1 egg
2 tablespoons canola oil
1 teaspoon vanilla extract
pinch of salt
⅓ cup confectioners' sugar
3 tablespoons all-purpose flour
1 tablespoon unsweetened
   cocoa powder
¼ teaspoon ground cinnamon
⅛ teaspoon ground cloves
2 egg whites
⅛ teaspoon cream of tartar
confectioners' sugar, to
   decorate
2 cups fresh raspberries, to serve

METHOD

1 Preheat the oven to 350°F. Generously coat 8 cups of a muffin pan with cooking spray. Sprinkle the teaspoon of sugar into the prepared cups, dividing it equally among them.

2 Put the chocolate and butter in the top of a double boiler set over simmering water, or use a heatproof bowl set over a saucepan of gently simmering water. Heat, stirring frequently, until the chocolate has completely melted.

3 To prepare the filling, combine the remaining tablespoon of sugar and the milk in a small saucepan and bring to a simmer. Cook, stirring frequently, until the sugar is completely dissolved. Stir in the corn syrup and about one-third of the melted chocolate (reserve the remainder for the cake batter) and stir until well combined. Chill in the freezer for about 30 minutes, or until firm.

4 To make the cake batter, combine the egg, oil, vanilla extract, and salt in a medium bowl and beat until well combined. Beat a bit of the egg mixture into the remaining chocolate until well blended. Mix the remaining egg mixture into the chocolate. Add the confectioners' sugar, flour, cocoa powder, cinnamon, and cloves and mix well.

5 In a large bowl, use an electric mixer set on medium speed to whisk the egg whites until frothy. Add the cream of tartar and continue to beat, gradually increasing the speed to high, until stiff peaks form. Gently fold the whipped egg whites into the batter.

6 Divide half of the batter evenly among the prepared cups of the muffin pan, placing about 1 heaping tablespoon in each. Spoon about a teaspoon of the chilled filling on top of the batter in each well. Spoon the remaining batter on top, dividing it equally. Make sure that the batter is fully covering the filling.

7 Bake in the preheated oven for 8–10 minutes, or until the edges begin to puff up. Remove the pan from the oven and place it on a wire rack to cool for several minutes.

8 Run a knife around the edge of each of the cakes, then place a cutting board over the top of the muffin pan and invert the pan, releasing the cakes. Dust the cakes lightly with confectioners' sugar and serve warm, topped with the raspberries.

Apricot & Chocolate Meringues

| calories 40 | fat 1.3g | sat fat 0.7g | total sugars 5.6g | carbs 6.5g |

INGREDIENTS
makes 12

6 apricots, halved and pitted
juice of ½ small orange
1 egg white
2 tablespoons superfine sugar
2 ounces semisweet chocolate,
    cut into 12 pieces

METHOD

1 Preheat the oven to 350°F.

2 Arrange the apricots, cut side up, on a baking sheet. Drizzle the orange juice over the top of them. Bake in the preheated oven for 5–8 minutes.

3 Meanwhile, whisk the egg white in a large, clean mixing bowl until you have stiff, moist-looking peaks. Gradually whisk in the sugar a teaspoonful at a time. Once all the sugar has been added, whisk for an additional 1–2 minutes, until the meringue is thick and glossy.

4 Spoon the meringue into a pastry bag fitted with a medium star tip. Put a piece of chocolate in the center of each apricot.

5 If the apricots wobble, stick them to the baking sheet with a little meringue. Pipe a whirl of meringue on top of the chocolate. Bake in the preheated oven for 5 minutes, or until the meringue is tinged golden brown and just cooked. Let cool for a few minutes, then transfer to a serving plate.

Mini Key Lime Pies with Quinoa Crust

| calories 137 | fat 3.6g | sat fat 1.7g | total sugars 14g | carbs 21.8g |

INGREDIENTS
makes 20
crust
cooking spray
1 cup quinoa
½ stick cold, unsalted butter,
　　cut into small pieces
½ teaspoon baking powder
¼ teaspoon salt
2 tablespoons cold water
2 tablespoons packed light
　　brown sugar

filling
2 eggs
2 egg whites
½ cup lime juice
finely grated zest of 1 lime
1 cup fat-free sweetened
　　condensed milk
½ cup nonfat plain yogurt

topping
2 egg whites
¼ cup granulated sugar
¼ teaspoon cream of tartar

METHOD

1 Preheat the oven to 350°F. Spray 20 cups of a 24-cup mini muffin pan with cooking spray.

2 To make the crust, put the quinoa in a food processor and process for about 7 minutes, until it is a fine powder (there will still be some whole kernels, which is fine). Add the butter, baking powder, and salt and process until the mixture resembles coarse bread crumbs. Add the water and brown sugar and process until the dough begins to clump.

3 Scoop about a tablespoon of the dough into each of the cups in the prepared muffin pan. Press the dough into an even layer in the bottom and all the way up the sides of each cup. Bake in the preheated oven for about 10 minutes, until lightly browned. Remove and set aside, but don't turn off the oven.

4 To make the filling, beat the eggs and egg whites in a large bowl with an electric mixer until well combined. Add the lime juice, lime zest, condensed milk, and yogurt and mix well. Spoon the mixture into the baked muffin shells, filling them almost to the top (you may end up with some leftover filling). Bake in the preheated oven for about 10 minutes, or until the filling is nearly completely set. Remove from the oven and let cool in the pan on a wire rack. Cover loosely with plastic wrap and chill for at least an hour.

5 To make the topping, preheat the oven once more to 350°F. Put the egg whites, sugar, and cream of tartar in a large bowl and beat with an electric mixer fitted with a whisk attachment on high speed until stiff peaks form. Transfer the topping to a pastry bag fitted with a large, star-shape tip. Pipe topping onto the center of each mini pie in a decorative peak. Bake in the preheated oven for about 10–12 minutes, or until the topping begins to brown. Transfer from the oven to a wire rack and let cool for about 15 minutes.

6 Run a knife blade around the edge of each pie to remove them from the baking pan. Serve warm or at room temperature.

Banana-Pecan Packages

calories 192 fat 5.2g sat fat 1.6g total sugars 20.6g carbs 31.7g

INGREDIENTS
serves 8
cooking spray
1 medium banana, mashed
¼ cup pecan pieces
3 tablespoons packed light
 brown sugar
16 square or round
 wonton wrappers
1 egg, beaten

sauce
1 tablespoon unsalted butter
½ cup firmly packed light
 brown sugar
2 tablespoons bourbon
 or other whiskey
⅓ cup whole milk
½ teaspoon vanilla extract

METHOD
1 Preheat the oven to 400°F. Line a large baking sheet with parchment paper and spray it with cooking spray.

2 In a medium bowl, combine the banana, pecan pieces, and brown sugar and stir to mix well. Lay out the wonton wrappers on your work surface and coat the edges with the beaten egg. Put 1 tablespoon of filling in the center of each wonton wrapper. Fold the wonton wrappers over to form semicircles or triangles and press to seal the edges. Transfer the wontons to the prepared baking sheet and bake in the preheated oven for about 5 minutes, or until crisp and lightly browned. Remove from the oven and let cool on the sheet while you make the sauce.

3 To make the sauce, combine the butter, brown sugar, and bourbon in a small saucepan set over medium–high heat. Cook, swirling the pan, until the sugar has completely dissolved. Add the milk and bring to a boil. Heat for another 5 minutes or so, until the mixture has thickened.

4 Remove from the heat and stir in the vanilla extract. Serve the wontons warm with the sauce drizzled over the top.

Pineapple Carpaccio with Mango Sauce

 calories 107 · fat 0.5g · sat fat 0.1g · total sugars 24g · carbs 25g

INGREDIENTS
serves 4

1 small pineapple
1 ripe mango
juice of ½ lime
½ cup fat-free plain yogurt

METHOD

1 Trim the top and bottom from the pineapple, then cut off all the skin and remove the "eyes." Use a large sharp knife to slice the pineapple into thin slices. Arrange the slices overlapping on a wide platter.

2 Peel, pit, and chop the mango flesh, then sprinkle with lime juice and use a blender or food processor to process to a smooth puree.

3 Put the mango puree in a small bowl. Spoon in the yogurt and swirl to create a marbled effect.

4 Put the bowl of mango sauce in the center of the platter. Serve the pineapple with the sauce spooned over the top.

Crème Caramel

calories
228

fat
3.3g

sat fat
1.6g

total
sugars
42.7g

carbs
42.7g

INGREDIENTS
makes 6

2 cups 2% milk
1 vanilla bean
½ cup plus ⅔ cup granulated
   sugar
⅓ cup water
2 eggs
4 egg whites
1 teaspoon vanilla extract

METHOD

1 Preheat the oven to 325°F. Set six ¾-cup ramekins (individual ceramic dishes) in a baking dish.

2 Pour the milk into a medium saucepan and set over medium heat. Split the vanilla bean lengthwise and, using the tip of a sharp knife, scrape out the seeds into the milk. Add the split bean to the milk. Heat until hot but not boiling. Remove from the heat and whisk in the ½ cup of sugar until it dissolves. Remove the vanilla bean and discard it. Set the milk mixture aside to cool.

3 In a small saucepan, combine the remaining ⅔ cup of sugar with the water and heat over low heat, swirling the pan occasionally, until the sugar has dissolved completely. Increase the heat to medium–high, bring to a boil, and cook, without stirring, until the mixture turns golden brown. Remove from the heat and divide among the ramekins so that it coats the bottom of each evenly.

4 In a large bowl, whisk together the eggs, egg whites, and vanilla extract. Slowly whisk the cooled milk mixture into the egg mixture. Ladle the mixture into the ramekins in the baking dish, dividing it equally. Pour boiling water into the baking dish to reach about halfway up the sides of the ramekins. Cover the baking dish with aluminum foil and bake for about 30 minutes, or until the custards are almost set. Remove from the oven and set the ramekins on a wire rack. Let cool for a few minutes, then chill in the refrigerator for at least 2 hours.

5 To serve, fill a shallow heatproof bowl with boiling water. Dunk the bottom of a ramekin in the hot water for a few seconds to loosen the caramel. Run a knife around the edge of the custard, place a dessert plate on top of the ramekin, and invert the plate so that the custard slips out. The caramel will run down the sides, creating its own sauce. Serve immediately.

Summer Fruit Upside-Down Cake

| calories 100 | fat 1g | sat fat 0.3g | total sugars 15g | carbs 20.5g |

INGREDIENTS
serves 12

cooking spray

2 firm, ripe peaches or nectarines, or 4 apricots or plums, pitted and sliced

¼ cup firmly packed light brown sugar

⅔ cup all-purpose flour

1 teaspoon baking powder

¼ teaspoon salt

2 eggs

1 egg white

½ cup granulated sugar

1½ teaspoons vanilla extract

METHOD

1 Preheat the oven to 375°F and spray a 10-inch round cake pan with 2-inch-high sides generously with cooking spray.

2 Put the sliced fruit into a medium bowl and sprinkle the brown sugar over it. Using your hands, gently toss the fruit so that it is well coated with the sugar. Arrange the fruit in a single layer in the prepared cake pan.

3 To make the batter, combine the flour, baking powder, and salt in a small bowl. In a large bowl, beat together the eggs, egg white, and sugar with an electric mixer, beginning on medium speed and gradually increasing the speed to high, for about 8 minutes, or until the mixture is pale yellow and fluffy. Add the vanilla extract and beat just to incorporate. Add the flour mixture in several additions and beat until just combined. Pour the batter into the cake pan on top of the fruit, using a rubber spatula to spread it in an even layer. Bake for 13–15 minutes, or until a toothpick inserted in the center of the cake comes out clean.

4 Let the cake cool in the pan for 2–3 minutes, then run a knife around the outside and turn it out onto a plate. Serve warm or at room temperature.

Index